PUZZLE
Pieces
of *Life*

Dr Gunta Krumins-Caldwell

It is with deep gratitude that I announce the existence of another piece of my heart, a book titled "The Gift of Grief and Loss: Courageous Care." This work encapsulates the raw emotions and profound experiences my family and I endured when faced with the daunting reality of terminal illness.

At the prime of our lives, my husband Ed and I found ourselves thrust into uncharted waters as he battled Motor Neuron Disease. With two young children to nurture and a burgeoning medical career, our world was rocked to its core. Despite the adversity, we embraced this journey as an opportunity for personal growth and communal learning.

However, what unfolded was a revelation of the complexities of human relationships in the face of mortality. Our altered circumstances strained the bonds with those closest to us, as many struggled to offer the care and support we desperately needed. In the shadow of such a relentless disease, the fragility of life became a palpable reality for all involved.

"The Gift of Grief and Loss: Courageous Care" serves as a poignant testimony to the resilience of the human spirit amidst adversity. Through the candid retelling of Ed, myself, and our children's experiences, readers are invited to explore their own capacity for empathy and understanding in the most trying of circumstances.

It is my sincerest hope that this book resonates with individuals who have faced loss or supported loved ones through illness. May it serve as a beacon of hope and compassion in times of darkness, illuminating the path towards profound connections and healing.

Ordering Information:

Prime Seven Media
518 Landmann St.
Tomah City, WI 54660

Printed in the United States of America

Dedication

To my precious family, my friends and my patients-all
of whom have been teachers to me in so
many different and rich ways

CONTENTS

Poems

These poems are forged by me, but not by me.
I have a wise guide that channels me well
So I could scribe the pain that we all feel
And give light to it all in good straight talk
So it gives us some insight of what we all feel
But also a chance to listen and learn
As we traverse this earth as best as we can
Given the stakes of handicaps big
But by giving a hand to each other,
We can elevate ourselves to alleviate some hurdles
To step into a world that is better by far

Finding You

I'll take you on a journey
Of curiosity and pain
Into the deeper layers of you,
Layer by layer,
From thinking,
To feeling,
To experiencing,
To realizing,
To acknowledging,
To eventually into
Your deep well of wisdom
That feels so rich
As you discover your true self
Ever deeper and deeper
Until surreptitiously
There is gratitude
Of self realised love
Of standing in your beauty 🧩

Enough

What is enough
We may well ask
Of ourselves and others
As we struggle to see
That enough is no friend
To the term mediocre.
So what is enough
As we struggle to see
That we are enough
Just as we are!
But that's not enough
It's frowned upon
And denigrated
As being just average
In a world of competitiveness
That surely falls short
Of what we 'should' expect
As we manoeuvre our way
Away from ourselves
And dishonour ourselves
To be what we are not
And forget to look within
To see our own treasures
That we feel are just rubbish
When we compare to another
As they struggle as well
To see their enoughness.

And so we seesaw
From enough
To average
To mediocre
To giving up on ourselves
As we try very hard
To see our own enoughness.
Yet that is life's point
That all that we need
And all our uniqueness
Is definitely ours
So how can we compare?
Better by far
To find within
The treasures we carry
And stamp them enough
And be glad that by going within
We eventually find
The gifts that are ours.
So carry them well
For they need you to see
That indeed
They are more than enough

Feminine

The days are all gone
When to flutter your eyelashes
And look all demure
Was the sign
Of the feminine
So gentle and pure
Where helplessness
Added to the demureness
Of woman
So sweet and succumbing
And so easy to suppress
But all through the ages
Below appearances so calm
A river has been flowing
And gathering speed
On its way to the sea
Enough has been endured
Enough has been pillaged
From this feminine being
As she rises to woman
But as she rises to woman
To feel her own strength
And establish her will
She gets accused of
The masculine
That isn't becoming
Of someone who
Nurtures

And takes care of the other
But how can Woman
Take care of another
If woman has never
Taken care of herself
So rise up woman
And learn what it takes
To cherish yourself
And to be yourself
In your strength and endeavors
For your feminine self
Needs introduction
On a level that defies
Any destruction
For your voice needs to be heard
And needs to find anchor
In a world that needs
Vision of the feminine manner
To balance our world
As it crumbles and falters
Let your river roar as it enters the sea
And becomes quite the balance
That needs to occur
For the world to be accepting
In the feminine and masculine
So that in mighty unison
Both can arise
And reflect the balance
Of the masculine and the feminine ❀

Masculine

He who wields a sword
Is mightier by far,
So lore has conveyed.
And if not by sword,
Then surely by force
And a voice to be heard,
As it bellowed and raged
Through the ages of time.
As it had a license
To do whatever it took
To feel strong, to protect
Or pillage and suppress
However it saw fit.
For some, it was good,
I'm sure of that,
But for others, it seemed it did not fit.
But how does a man take off a mantle
That has been impressed
On the being we call man?
As boys do not cry,
Oh, what a shame
That this was such a mantra
For man to comply.
And man struggles
To find his own place
In a world that is changing
And no step feels sure.

To find that strength
And express it so gently
Seems such a contradiction
With the mantle one wears.
But under that mantle
Is a man with a heart
That hadn't, till now,
Been allowed to express.
For surely, the heart
Is anything but manly.
But without the feelings
That express through our heart,
Man cannot discover
The joy and the wonder
That feelings can bring.
But it's a battle for sure,
So deep and profound,
That needs the feminine
To bring it around.
Both need to step up
To balance this wrong
And to find in each other
What alone cannot be found. ❧

Forgiveness

Ah forgiveness
That ubiquitous word
That gets thrown around
Without it's true meaning
Being targeted well.
We can forgive
But never forget
So they say.
But is that it's true meaning
Or just a glib fashion
Ah but one must forgive
But dare not forget
Just in case
We are faced with the same
Yet again
But if that's the case
Surely it means
The lesson's not learned
And Grace is not found
As we judge how it is
And struggle to find
The means to forgive
When it can't be our fault
Although it takes two.
For how did it happen
That I couldn't see
That real forgiveness
Is just so elusive

Where squirming
To go within
And see what it shows
That's triggered me so
That it needed a finger
Pointed at the other,
Not seeing the three
That were pointing at me.
But judging another
Means judging ourselves
And there lies the trap.
To not truly forgive
Until we can see the trigger in us
We will keep on judging
And yearning forgiveness
Allowing to satisfy
This beast within
That hankers forgiveness
As it must be fed
From always without.
But being fed from within
We need to discover
What makes it so hard
To forgive our true selves 🧩

Anger

Why are you angry?
Oh such a silly question!
To someone whose angry
As all can be witness to.
Why ask the question
When the answer is clear
To someone whose anger
Must be a screen.
Suddenly it's clear to them
As the fear is baiting them.
But anger is screening it,
That overwhelming fear
But the mind is succumbing
To express it as fear
But it all seems too frightening
As the fear is encompassing
And refuses to leave,
As it courses through
Body that feels so rigid
That it feels such a chore
In mind and in body.
To wish it to go
Would create such relief,
But it is so unrelenting
And sticky and close.
Why can't it leave
So living can happen
And the cause of the fear

Can be left unattended?
So anger can resume its place
Without being usurped
By a fear attended
To give deep relief
With some understanding
Where this fear is living
In a body so closed
That requires deep love
To prise it wide open
And deal with the fear
That till now
Was unspoken
Apart from as anger 🧩

What are the odds?

What are the odds
Of something happening?
People will ask
As they ponder the dilemma,
As if the question in play
Is a gamble indeed.
What are the odds
That she'll meet
The man of her dreams,
Or worse still,
That someone recovering
Against all odds
Is just a game of Russian roulette?
And all that's at play
Is just the roll of a dice!
What are we seeing
If all that it seems
Is just a life that is chance?
When maybe there is fecundity
In this complex arena
That some of us call
The Earth School of Life.
Maybe there are insights
That need to be discovered
When we roll a dice
And a prize is expected.

Maybe the prize
Is far more elusive
As we hope for the chance
That turns up so differently
Than how we expected.
Maybe there are insights
That need to be seen.
Maybe there are lessons
To experience,
So that we may discover
In this Earth School of Life
What is deep inside us
That needs to be seen
And needs to transmute
To something more meaningful
Than we thought possible
That takes courage
And temerity, I know,
And it's surely much more
Than a roll of a dice.
For in our deep delving
That seems hard to stomach,
We may find some answers
That are pure magic,
And the chance of a lifetime
To truly discover
A part of ourselves
Is better by far
Than a roll of a dice
That gives us a sense
That life is all but a chance 🧩

Procrastination

Dear procrastination,
We could write you a letter
And let you know first hand
How we have been fairing
In this sorry state of self.
But procrastination already knows,
To move out of the trenches
That seem to get deeper
The longer we stay
In that inert state
Is anything but easy,
And the fatigue
Is overwhelming,
And the inertia that binds us
To that trench floor
Is astounding.
It's like a magnet
That keeps on pulsating
To make sure we stay there
And give it a meaning.
But in a trench lonely
Our soul is not fed,
But it's safe down there,
Even though
We may be starving,
Starving for sustenance
Vibrancy of life.

But how do we move
When the magnet is pulsating
And holding us back?
It may take sheer effort
To extricate oneself
From this inertia state.
But effort is rewarding,
Just give it a try,
And suddenly you find
You are free of the trenches.
This maybe scary
As well as new,
But every small action
Is a step in the right direction.
Don't belittle yourself
For the steps maybe small,
But sooner or later
The trench is no more
Of the time when you thought
There is never a chance.
But look what happens
When you take a chance on you
And find yourself smiling
With deep satisfaction
On what has been gained
Through effort
Astounding 🧩

Alone/Lonely

Alone is misinterpreted
As it is seen by most
Surely as a state full of loneliness,
Yet being alone
Can be liberating
And oh so empowering,
Quite the opposite of lonely,
Which is cloaked in deep fear.
Lonely is finding solace in media
And making as much noise
As our psyche can handle.
Lonely is being in a room full of people
And finding ourselves
In a deep state of fear,
For how can it be
That in a room full of people
Inside there can be
Just a deep state of empty?
If we have the courage
To feel this deep Loneliness,
Then to know this state
Is a disconnect of self
That is desperately seeking
The solace in distraction.
But taking our gaze in a different direction
Is avoiding the solace
Of deep reflection.

But reflection requires doggedness
To not avoid,
To delve inside ourselves and
Through all the crevices
Seek ourselves out
To find
That part of the you
That will give us the gumption
To sit with ourselves
And find that we have
Good company to keep.
For then we have arrived
At a place of content
To hold our own hand
And admire ourselves.
How lovely it is
To spend time with just you 🧩

Responsibility

Take responsibility
So we are told,
But what does that mean
In this world of ours
Where responsibility
Could leave us out in the cold
As everyone struggles
Within themselves
To be true to some part of them
Yet comply to the crowd?
Complying is safe
It keeps us enclosed
In a blanket of comfort
That feels just so right
But right can feel tight
If we reflect deep enough
To see that it's not
The uniqueness of us
But the fear of others
We can call the collective.
And the fear within
Stepping out on our own
To own what's for us
Can seem rather strange
As well as without comfort,
As the fear of being different
Blasts in our ears.

And then we succumb
Again to the noise
Of the crowd all around us
As we look and view,
But try to extricate
That part of ourselves
That has the courage
To not take note
Of the whispers
And looks
That seem to be impacting.
If we choose to see
What others dare not,
As we step tentatively
On new ground for us
And feel the peace
That comes with the joy
Of taking responsibility
For some part of ourselves

Mirror Mirror

Some people stare
At their own reflection
In a mirror so murky
It is hard to make out
As they peer and squint and to stare
At this reflection
They can barely conjure up
And ask in all earnestness
Mirror mirror on the wall
Who is the fairest of them all
And if the mirror could speak
And satisfy their question
Are hoping against hope
That the mirror would say
That they are ok
And nothing to do
And there would be relief
With a sigh indeed
That gives them a false illusion
That nothing's to be done
As it's just who they are
And the ego feels satisfied
That this self reflection
Of digging in deep
Is all just some nonsense
That is meant to upset
A perfectly held stance
And the ego was right

To just sit tight
And stare straight ahead
At the long narrow road
And feel very comfortable
That they are certain for sure.
Because the narrowness shows
A clear path ahead
And then there is no disputing
In the ego's mind and head
Where to place the next step
As it's easy to see
When the road is so narrow.
But the deflection is real
Even though the fear is not palpable
That to delve into mind waters
That are anything but safe
Would require an openness of mind
That would feel most definitely
As doom is impending
Of a magnitude so great
That it's best to keep the mirror
All murky and dull.
But all around them are people
Whether partner or friend
Or colleague indeed
In all kindness and compassion
Can see that their narrowness of road
Is not serving well
This person who seems
Quite content to just be
On this very narrow journey
That gives them direction

That feels safe and steady
And yes, it takes much courage
To spin around
And look at the past road
So narrow and safe
And be completely honest
If they dare be so
To see that this road could be
Widened indeed
To explore more options
That could serve them more broadly.
But they cringe and become
Quite arrogant indeed
And defensive in look
And can't see without collapsing
And imploding in self
That they are quite comfortable
Just where they are now
And to rock the boat
Would cause drowning for certain.
And that's not an option
That they are prepared for
And miss quite the point
That metaphorically speaking
A drowning may mean
A new way of looking
Having let go of the old 🧩

Settling for less

Settling is such a neutral action
So bland and so vanilla
It really requires
A kick to the psyche.
Who wants to settle
And live a bland life
Where everything seems
So vanilla and nice?
And for less-
My goodness
Seems such a waste
To think that's the best
That life has to offer.
Surely there is more
For this life to bring.
But maybe it's others
Who have tapped into that.
It seems so easy
No rocking the boat
If we stay in Settleville
And feel quite at home.
But what does it take
To open the gates
And walk right out
Of the Settleville estate?
It takes tenacity
Or a crisis maybe
To shake us all out
Of this stupefied state.

But thank you for that
For without that big push
I doubt very much
Whether most would acknowledge
The state they were in
Was anything but exhilarating,
Joyous or fun.
But safe abates fear
And keeps it at bay
For who knows what would happen
If the gates were flung open.
But prise that stiff lock
That has rusted to still
And bound past the gates
No holding you back.
Feel the liberation
That freedom allows
And see what mischief
Life beholds for you now.
When you realise
That sensation,
That liberation brings
Will suffice your needs
When exhilaration shows
There are challenges to be had
On this journey outside.
But oh it's so worth it
There is not a doubt.
For now vanilla has turned to a
Kaleidoscope of experiences rich.
Who could have known
If we settled for less
And thought vanilla was nice? 🦋

There are no ordinary moments

There are no ordinary moments,
So Socrates says
In Dan Millman's book.
It may seem esoteric,
But let me explain
That a smile
Can bring warmth to a heart,
A heart that a moment before
Was weighted in sorrow.
We never do know
What an ordinary moment
Could bring to us all
That suddenly becomes
Not so ordinary
After all.
Each moment brings
A reflection to all,
But can we be vigilant
And catch it at all?
But if we are ready to see
It has magic,
We might just discover
A glimpse of another,
A world full of wonders.

Just open your eyes
And take in the scrumptioness
Set out before.
But if it so seems
That it is anything but joy,
We can also reflect
That not all life's moments
Are meant to be that
Joyous or full of our wants.
But maybe, just maybe
That difficult moment is just what we need
To heed
The cry of our sorrowing heart
That wants to stride forward
And learn what it can
In each moment of time.
So satisfied it can feel
And replenished in self
For it grasped each moment
To walk in it's field
And live its fill.
So it could be satiated
That it had done it well
To cherish each moment
As best that it could

Regret

Regret - such a sad emotion,
All standing forlorn
With its head in a bow.
Regret feels so heavy
And woeful and bad
As if there is
No escape from its clutches.
Regret seems so final
So desperate and down
As if there is no tomorrow.
Is it surely so final?
Regret seems so pity full
All laden down
And carrying itself
With a frown, no doubt
Where the mind
It goes back and forth
Ruminating it seems
On what could have been
Or how should it be.
Yet in all this regret
Our energy is wasted
For watching our mind
Go back and forth
Can never resolve
What has been done and dusted.

But learn we can surely
From what did occur
And step up and claim
Our part in the regret.
For as we step up
And claim what is ours
We can learn in this space
And feel the lightness of pace
That comes from facing
Our part in regret.
And as we face this terrible foe
Realise our foe
Is but ourselves
For being so harsh
On our regretful selves.
When turning around
And resolving to claim
That to drop regret
We must learn to see
What is ours alone,
To lessen our load
And strive to observe,
What burdened us so,
That landed us in
A place of regret 🧩

Sympathy Empathy and Compassion

The story it goes
That there are three friends
Who meet in a bar
On a regular date
To discuss and have a laugh
About what is the state
Of their respective namesakes
That keep wandering around
The streets of this earth.
And two seem quite lost
Their names are well known,
For most people believe
They are quite sure of
What the meaning is
Of these three friends.
Sympathy wants to muscle right in
And tell the two others
What it really means
To have sympathy for another.
It is such a hard task
Both Empathy and Compassion
Nod in unison and agree
That being sympathetic
Is no easy gig.
Sympathy jumps into

Every arena
And feels every pain
Disappointment and strain
And feels quite exhausted
After such an endeavour
To gather itself
For the onslaught of another.
But Sympathy
Is finding it difficult
To understand the concept
That stepping into the fire
With another
Is no help at all
To the helpless sufferer.
Now Empathy steps in
And explains quite clearly
That it's way is better
And far less taxing
Because it doesn't need
To step into the fire
To be of sincere help
To listen to the other
But it does take some effort
Empathy has to agree
To remain quite impartial
Can be quite the strain
It has to admit.
But it's certainly better
Than trying to help,
The way Sympathy thinks
Is the only way through.

Now both Sympathy
And Empathy
Are in quite a discussion
And not much is heard
From their friend named Compassion.
But suddenly both turn
To their wise friend to see
As the silence is becoming
Quite definite and resounding.
Compassion looks earnest
At one and then the other
And says quite clearly
In a voice
That speaks heart
In every word spoken,
And says quite gently,
But with its distinct authority,
There is no doubt
That its place is clear.
For all it must do
Is be witness to each action
And allow the ailing other
To have voice to their dilemma
Without giving opinion
Or feeling their pain.
For then the other
Is free to discover
What may work for them
As their empowerment grows.

They are able to decipher
In their troubled state
What could be the answer.
But Sympathy wants to hug
The sad sod it seems,
And Empathy wants
To be known that it's listening,
And so again,
Both Sympathy and Empathy
Walk away from Compassion
And realise yet again
There is still work to be done
To be like Compassion
That takes years of insight
To get to a place
Where just being witness
Is the most graceful state 🧩

Curiosity

Desmond Tuti once said
We need to stop pulling people
Out of the river
And go upstream
And find out why
They are falling in so.
But to do such a trek,
Which requires much effort,
We would first have to
Switch on our curious nature,
With a switch that's quite stuck
In a dimmer light switch
That hasn't been turned
And manoeuvred in a awhile.
Curiosity requires a sense of enquiry
And gumption -what's that?
To forge a path to go up the river,
Which would definitely mean
Forging upstream against
The tide of the masses ⚘

Cause

So cause is the enigma
That life has to offer,
For I have been taught
Many moons in the past
By teachers much wiser by far,
That unless cause is found,
It is truly not worth
Putting a label
On we know not what.
Cause is the enigma
That leaves us in despair,
As all one wants to do
Is label it thus,
For putting a label on
Seems safe and secure,
That we can then all
Surely review
What the label is for.
But my curious mind
Won't let me be still
Until I can discover
The cause underneath.
But not many want to move
From this place so secure,
For labels are language
We all adhere to.
But I want to know
What caused it so,

And not be afraid
If I don't understand,
Or discover a world
That seems fresh and new,
Where cause is all
Wonder and might.
For in looking for cause,
I am open to find
A world that is bigger by far
That what I could see
As I struggled with label
That didn't just fit.
But courage is needed
To rip off the label
And see a Band-Aid
And, oh what might it carries!
For the stifling fact
That label can bring
An arrogance broad
That fits all labels
But stifles the mind
In narrowness great
Without the growth
That discovery needs.
So then there is wither and shrivel
In minds not so great.
Take off the hat
That's sitting so tight
That gives the impression
That everything's right,

And dare to look deeper
Past what has been taught
And realise so humbly
That what was taught stridently
May be a view
That helped keep us all
In blindness and in good check 🧩

Passion

I believe it is passion
As we immerse into life
And feel the rhythm of its pulse
And feel the seduction of its sound.
Can you feel the sensuality of life?
It's calling to you.
It's calling you forth
To immerse in its womb,
To follow its flow,
To feel it's deep essence,
As you fall into line
With wind through your hair
And the sun on your finger tips.
Can you feel the earth's pulse
As your feet sink into Gaia?
Listen to the trees
As they whisper to you
For they know the wisdom
That comes with the silence
Of standing quite still.
Yet it's leaves are a rustle
That defies any instrument
With its myriad of sounds.
Feel the roar of the ocean
As it blasts its force
In the form of a wave,
As it hits the sand hard
And tells you aloud,

I am a force to be reckoned with!
Can you follow my lead?
The power I have
Is a power you have
If you unleash
Your life force
As you blast into life.
Can you do what I do
Without inhibition
No matter the cost?
For cost will only be
If you hold yourself back
For fear of retribution
That comes with being unique
In our world of conformity
That belies its own creation.
Can you seduce yourself enough
To mesmerise doubt,
To follow your heart
Like the rain feeds our need
To be watered and nourished
So the parchment of fear
Can be washed into Gaia.
And instead rise up
Like a phoenix through laughter
As you feel the true self
That took so long
To bloom into flower.
But look at it now
In its sensual glow
Radiating out
Like the glow from the sun

Blinding in strength
Yet radiating warmth.
Feel the calling it brings
In your muted heart
That the ego has silenced
For far too long.
Rise up and bring heart
To where it belongs
To voice your longing
That's been buried for far too long.
And let your heart sing its song
So it can be heard
As a roar on the wind
As it kisses the cheek
And is embraced in the knowing
That comes with a tear ❁

Boundaries

In the frontiers of the mind
Partitions are created
To ineptly denote
That's important to establish
And make the demarcation clear
That there is no stepping over
This very clear line
For one purpose indeed
To protect one's great ego
That thinks that a boundary
Is solving the matter.
Boundaries is such a misunderstood term
In the vernacular of the psyche.
It is conveyed to give us space,
So don't you overstep
My precious ground.
There is a line in the sand
That is marked quite clearly,
That stepping past it
Is laden with retribution.
For it is stated quite emphatically,
That this in the stand
That marks the boundary line.
And when it comes to mind,
Let us be very clear
That my mind is quite sensitive
To many a topic
That are not to be raised.

For my boundary states,
Then you would be overstepping the line.
But in creating a boundary
One is not prepared to suffer
To understand the triggers
That then require a boundary.
Boundary means safety
And no interaction
To find the real reason
That the boundary matters.
Drop all the posts
That make up a boundary
And look at what's needed
To clear such a ground.
For that boundary is there for one reason
And one reason only.
It seems all too hard
To look in the mirror
And see what is creating this need.
For this boundary so justly it seems,
Is doing the job of standing guard,
So that one doesn't have to
Look at what's confusing
And creating a whirl,
Because we are told that
Boundaries are healthy.
If there is danger in staying
Then boundaries are useless
And what one needs to do
Is leave the place promptly.

But if it is triggers
That irritate us so,
Then the only wise action
Is dive right in and discover
What it is we find hard
To stand without boundaries,
And scour the ground
That seems too rocky and unstable.
But clearing some mind debris
May make such a difference
To seeing more reasonably
That what was so rocky
Was only the fact
That there wasn't a clearing.
Clearing our mind
Of some past events
Will show quite succinctly
That the boundaries we thought
Were keeping us quite safe
Were in actual fact
Hedging us in 🧩

Death

Death is a presence
No point in denying
As it lurks in the corridors of our fumbling minds.
Creating such shadows
As it flits and it flirts
And teases us on
To we know not when.
And it seems so ubiquitous
As we battle to align
Our perception of time
With the reality of its drum.
As we struggle to milk the best
Of the space
That we call life.
Death gives a jolt
When it lands on another,
And we cry tears of sorrow,
For it seems so unfair
That it happened just then.
And we struggle to
See it's beauty in life,
For it can seem so final indeed.
Yet we fail to see
That it's teaching us life
To be grateful to live
In this wonderful state.

And the more we can taste
The moment we have,
The more we can taste
The true essence of life.
It shows us our weaknesses
As well as our strengths
To evolve as we gather
The lessons of life
To make us the wiser
For being here and now 🧩

Lazy

Lazy- such a languid action
Full of guilt and despair.
It depicts useless and worthless
Or so we are told.
But peer underneath
And have a closer view
At what's happening to lazy.
As others judge and despise,
Lazy is curled into a tight ball
Not knowing what to do.
It feels impotent and stuck
And paralysed and frightened.
When lazy is your label
There is nothing to do
For that in itself
Makes any action too hard.
So frightened is it
To make the wrong move
That being called lazy
Is an easier cue.
Maybe lazy needs some help
To see its own worth
To encourage it so
And allow it to flourish
In ways that may be
Different than ours.

It needs to see
The value it has
By looking within
To see what it values
And to add weight to its value
By supporting itself
Looking deep within
And discarding such an action
To find underneath
There can be satisfaction
In what is discovered
When we become completely deaf
To the label of lazy

Kind

Be kind they say,
It's blasted everywhere
From PA systems
In shopping centre malls
Be kind they say
From flashing screens
Everywhere.
Oh how banal is that
That we need to be
Reminded it seems
Twenty four seven
In case we forget
As the human race we are
That seems to have forgotten
What kindness is about
In this new age of ours.
And no doubt we are irritated
By this and by that,
But just blasting out 'be kind'
Will not stop the bleed
Of our wounded selves
As we struggle
To be kind to our troubled selves.
How can we be kind
When we falter so,
And if we are honest
Within ourselves
We wouldn't know how.

For we humans it seems
Are good at focusing on fault
In ourselves
As we view us and others
Through
A critical lens
And give credit to this lens
That is quite warped, I might add
As it appears to be rather opaque.
So it's pointed out sincerely
Which gives us a jolt
As we hadn't assessed
This dirty lens of ours
In quite some time now.
But even with this blurry
lens of ours
We seem to trust it more
Than the positive lens.
For what this lens shows is
We have fogged it up well
And to explore our selves deeper
To see what the cause
That our lens wants to show
And give us the doubtful feedback
Of lots of deep faults
Which our soul wants to reject.
But with deep reflection
We can take off this lens
That has kept us small
In our lack of kindness to all.
So dig deep and find what
Gives us the illusion

That negative talk
Works well on yourself
Until you can find
Your kindness for self.
Then the PA systems
And blaring flashing bright screens
Will feature no more
In a world filled with
Kindness to all ✿

Respect

Respect what's that?
In this new world order of ours
Where the catch cry
Of me, me, me
Has squeezed respect out.
Respect bowed and exited
Quite some time back now,
As it didn't feel it's rightful place
Was here and now
In this shattered world of boundaries galore
It seemed it was not being seen
In this crowded new space
Where everyone feels
That they have a right
To show their importance of self.
And rightly so!
As we have been through ages
Where children should be seen
And not heard
That now all of a sudden everyone feels
That to have a voice
And make sure it's heard
Is going to heal the past trauma no doubt
And so the pendulum swings
To the other extreme
So that one can learn
How this voice does sound.

But dear child of our times
We must all reflect
That putting ourselves first
May not really work
For then we cause alienation and much more
As we find the tribe that answers our call.
But that just stifles us
All well and good
If we want to be heard
And validated more.
But that's not the world
We are all aiming to score
As that puts us in capsules
As a tight squeeze for all.
And all these capsules
Feel comfortable for sure
But don't knock into me
I'm warning you now
For your capsule it seems
Doesn't fit with mine
It's easy to see.
So how can I respect you
If you can't see me in mine
So respect must be called back
To sort out the mess
And disperse all our capsules
As we gasp with deep fright.
But respect is quite firm
That in order to evolve
We need all see the other
And delve inside of us
To find all the triggers

Of traumas long past
That put us in capsules to protect us
We thought.
But living side by side
In a conciliatory manner
Brings hope to the human race
As we are guided by respect
As it works it's magic
And gives us all hope
Of a far better tomorrow

Arrogance

Excuse me, arrogance
Could I have a word with you, please?
I would just like to know
What drives you so
That you have the floor
Above all others?
You seem to think
That you know a lot,
And I bow to you deeply
If that is the case.
But it is hard to imagine,
In this day and age,
That that is possible at all
When we are flooded with so much.
But there is no doubt
That it may appear so
That chasing a stream
Of rich information
On our burgeoning internet
Would give the impression
That that could be so.
But it really depends on what tunnel we take.
If that doesn't happen to be
What they call
A rabbit hole indeed
That validates your beliefs
That were already quite set,
Just needed confirmation,

That the internet met
But maybe you are forgetting,
Or choosing not to see,
That the internet is a whirl pool of stuff
That may seem to give you the answers
You would like,
But not necessarily
What's what.
As a shift is happening
Right now,
For the times are a changing,
So the song seems to go.
And maybe, just maybe
It's not as it seems.
But when we have been taught
By the elite, as we denote
It seems
So hard to extricate self
From a paradigm
That seemed to validate quite nicely
All that you were taught and know.
For the fear must be great
To step off the tracks
And follow a route that was
Quite set
And tentatively change tracks
That seems scary as hell.
And look all around you
At the bleak surrounds
As there are few to be found
On this stark horizon
Of new beginnings.

But as you explore
This unfamiliar territory
And are ready to accept
That what you do know
May seem far fetched, as you open your heart
And let go of fear
That may be, just maybe
Your arrogance may slightly -oh gosh
Be able to embrace
A thought process
So new
That you may be astounded
When you step back and view
That your arrogance was just a mask
For your own fears and doubts
That what seemed so real
Is not really so
And with heart wide open
It is easier to see
That options are exciting
On this new terrain
And eyes wide open
And ears just listening
A peace may descend
On those shoulders of yours
That were quite rigid and defensive
A stance that now seems
So narrow for all.
How humbling is that? 🧩

Fear

What is fear
But love upside down?
Or can love be
The foil to fear?
Our brain cannot conjure
Both at the same time.
But sadly it defaults
To that hind brain of ours
And have us behave
From our reptilian brain.
Although it can be quite subtle
And quite the sneak,
For it can masquerade as love
When much is at stake.
Our life is fear- driven
Please be witness to that.
For fear can allude
In the most curious of manner.
Fear can offer us
Safety it seems
To hide in its underwing
And feels quite content
To give us the impression
That we are safe.
Yet fear distorts
And gives the perception
That we need to be vigilant
And colder than ice.

For in so being
We may escape the pain
That feels inescapable
If we let go of fear
Which requires much,
As fear is so convincing,
But letting go mindfully
Will allow love to prevail
And our frontal lobe to shine
In a way that
Try as we might
Our reptilian brain
Can never achieve. 🧩

Time

Where were you, time
When I needed you so?
Where were you, time
When I had forgotten?
Why didn't you remind me
That you are so precious?
What was I doing
When you kept on marching?
Where did you go
When I tried to hold on
To this nebulous state
That we call time?
You didn't listen,
You didn't heed
To my pleas and my wants
When I tried so hard
To plead with you earnestly
And became quite cross
That you didn't slow down
No matter my frown.
So eventually I learned
That time has no ear.
It has its own pace
For me to surrender
To its graceful flow
And to step into line
As it beats its own rhythm
For me to allow.

And all I can do
Is be in the moment
To cherish it sincerely
As time continues on. 🧩

Mistake

Mistake is a word
That needs to be gone
From our everyday language.
Oh, it is so harsh
And misses the point
Of how we can manage
Our life in this world
When we are so human.
Our lessons, our friend
As we travel through life
On a bender of travails
That have their own agenda
We need to embrace.
Mistakes it can't be
Unless we succumb
To the terrible view
That we are just that
And no space for change.
But mistake is an experience
That if worthy
Of living-
It's wisdom to know
If we just immerse
In the depth of its learning,
If we so dare.
For in diving in deep
In this stuckness of muck
We can rise from its depths

Wiser by far
And lighter I'm sure,
Having gained the sight
That experience brings
When we dare find the jewel
In the essence of life
That we demean
By calling a mistake,
When in truth
We are richer by far
For having just gone through
Something so profound
That has left us wiser and richer
No doubt. &

Time heals

Time heals-
So they say.
Time erases our yesterday-
So they say.
But wounds leave scars,
Nothing to say.
Scars are hard
No question there.
So has the wound gone,
Or is it just buried
Under the hardness of yesterday?
Has time healed,
Of just made us resilient
To weather more
Of what life seems to offer?
I guess the best we can do
Is learn from our wounds
To follow our heart
To soften those scars
To always remind us
That we have survived
And so we can see
A reflection,
A reflection of who we can be.
For in our wound is our healing
If we so choose. 🧩

Triune of Life

The triune of life
Is the balance between
Your masculine and feminine.
As the two come into balance
At the opposite angles of
Of the triangle's essence
They strive to reach higher
As they delve in deeper
That leads them both
To yearn
To a higher consciousness indeed.
For the Infinite or Divine
Which is the point of the triangle
That sits well above
The masculine and feminine.
In this triangle there is emptiness
And in this great emptiness
There is deep enormous fullness
With the riches of life.
And with this fullness of life
We can live in the moment

Ubuntu

'I am because we are'
Is a Nguni Bantu expression
And the thought is deep
As it's true meaning is fraught
With a term we may banter
But escapes our mere thought.
It means Humanity no less
To give us the meaning
That seems to escape us:
That we cannot exist
If we don't cooperate well
As a team standing together.
Just like in nature,
Everything is connected
And can't be separated,
For individuation in Nature
Is a anathema of sorts,
As it is not possible
To stride out alone.
As a tree by itself
Will never survive,
It needs birds
It needs sun and of course the rain,
And the fungi beneath
Is connecting the roots
To make it all function
In a homeostatic state.

And that is what Ubuntu
Is all about:
Aknowledging self
As well as the other.
But that seems to take
A learning indeed
In this western world of ours,
Where we don't even pause
To reflect on our world,
Complex as it is.
It couldn't exist
If the garbage wasn't removed
And the trains just stopped running
And our online shopping
Came to a screeching halt.
But it all takes humanity
To keep it ticking along.
Just like in Nature,
Everything needs respect
And acknowledged
As important.
For who can imagine
A tree saying no
To the fruit that it's grown
For the taking?
But let's recognise its efforts
As it strives to produce,
That then we can devour
With not even a thought
Of what that took
To get the fruit to market,

So we may select
All we could want.
If we just began
To integrate Ubuntu
In our sorry state,
We may find it astounding
How this could feel inside.
For to see me in you
And you in me too
Could give us deep gratitude
For our separated selves
And give us the temerity
Of thought
That you and me both
Can bow to each other 🧩

Smile

They say that the eyes
Are the windows to the soul,
And I say a smile,
Is the door to the heart
A smile conveys so much
Depending on how
That smile is expressed
And launched into space.
For a smile has many variations
Of how it projects
Into the surrounds
That it spills into.
It can seem loud and excited
As teeth flash with it
In happiness spilling
Right out that heart door.
But then of course,
The smile can be
All demure and quite shy,
As the door to the heart
Is ajar just slightly,
For it is not too sure
If it should smile some more
Or just leave you guessing
What's behind that door.
But there is nothing quite like it
When the smile is so genuine
That there is no doubt

That the door is wide open
And inviting you in
With a smile of your own.
As the energy of smiles
Can be so infectious
And lead to some laughter
As the eyes dance
Brightly
As they mix with the smile
And radiate this beauty
That two smiles can bring
To a place once so empty.
But a smile can be sad
With a reminiscence on its lips
As it reflects on a past memory
That seems bitter sweet.
For the smile may convey
That the memory is lovely
But the time is no more
And that brings the smile
A tinge of sadness indeed.
Then there is the smile
That a parent has for its child,
And there are no words to describe
A smile such as this,
For it displays deep affection
But protection as well,
As it's adoring smile
Alights the child's face,
And both are in deep reflection
As the adoring is mutual
And defies any distraction.

And what about lovers
Who have eyes only for each other?
And their smile conveys
Such a deep love of the other
That knocking on that door
Will be deaf to the ears
Of two lovers entwined
In their thundering love.
For their smile for each other
Is like a wall
To the world outside
That no amount of knocking
Will stop their eyes locking
As their smiles connect
Only for each other.
But many more smiles
Are needed in this ailing world
That feels so disconnected
And so afraid to connect.
But connection is imperative
If we are to move forward
And bring a different world
To this sad place of ours.
It's all very well
To have smiles for your friends
Or lovers or family.
But we need smiles
That blanket this planet
And show it the love
That can come with a smile.
If all doors are flung open
And we embrace one another

And drop all our fears
As we connect with one another
And feel the warmth
Coursing through
All the doors of humanity
As our eyes begin to dance
And our hearts start to pound
To the beauty that such a smile
Brings to each other 🧩

Expectations

Expectations seem thrilling
When we conjure up dreams
Of how things will be
And gaze into space,
As we wonder and smile
At how things will work out.
For how could they not!
We have dreamt it so well
How it will be
And so it should be.
But then all of a sudden
Our dreams go awry
And what we had dreamt
Is no longer fact.
Oh why did it shatter
This great expectation?
It seemed so well planned,
It's execution sure,
Yet then life took over
And all was so different
Than what was expected.
We frown and we cry
And lament about plans
That didn't go
Accordingly.
Oh why couldn't it be so
The way it was meant?
And yet the retort

Is clear as a bell.
Why should things go
According to plan,
When going awry
Gives us a chance
To reflect on our
Dreams
That seem to
Evaporate
As life takes the reins
And makes plans of its own.
That doesn't seem fair
And doesn't seem right
That what had been dreamt
Will not come to light.
Yet we miss a great piece
Of learning indeed
If we think that our plans
Should be set in concrete.
Life is just teaching us
That letting go well
Will give us the space
To acknowledge the realms
That we couldn't imagine
Until life shifted gears
And gave us the sight
To see things quite differently
Than ever thought possible.
And if we are humble
And can bow to this Grace
We are bound to see life
With a different face.

And there is the wisdom
The insight as well
That viewing more broadly
Can give us the lesson
That will be more
Grounding than
Mere dreams of our own. ❧

At odds with oneself

Oh, it's such a dilemma
When we are
At odds with ourselves,
As our clashing thoughts
Keep bashing each other
And reverberating so
In our cavernous mind.
As our thoughts echo wildly
In our chamber of mind,
And we can't think clearly
As our thoughts are so unruly,
Like undisciplined children,
All running amok,
As they push and shove
And elbow for space,
Not knowing where or how,
As they keep running around
In this mind of ours.
And no matter the attempts
Of settling them down,
They seem to gather pace
And start screaming,
"Oh, for heaven's sake!"
And we can feel quite distraught
As we observe this scene play out,
As no sense can be made
Of this undisciplined mess,
Not knowing which thought

To discipline first,
And becoming quite exhausted
And dismayed about it all.
But try as we might,
We don't seem to achieve
That quietness of mind
With these unruly thoughts.
So going to sleep,
Or taking a pill,
Or spending up big
And having a few too many
Seems always the solution
To helping ourselves
By distracting
From our chattering thoughts.
But then eventually we awake,
And we are deflated so,
When these undisciplined thoughts
Are watching us still,
To start once again
Running and clashing about
And being way too loud.
"Oh, damn and bother!
What to do now!"
But a way must be found
To discipline this whole mess,
And it may be deep breathing
Or saying a mantra,
Meditation may help,
Or a walk in deep nature.
We can find the elixir
That can help us begin

To herd these thoughts
To a more peaceful place
That will console our being
And be calmer in thought,
And give us the impetus
To steady our minds.
So being at odds with ourselves
Will be a thing of the past. 🧩

Spite and retribution

Spite and retribution
Are having it out
To oppress the other
With a fiery exchange,
For the best way is theirs
To express their deep hurt
That it seems was flung on to them
With a dagger so deep
That it left a wound exposed,
Oh, so profoundly indeed.
Spite wants their victim to feel
How much agony is writhing within,
And retribution is gunning it,
For how dare someone malign them so,
It needs to be addressed,
So they are redressed,
Oh, so much anger flashing,
Eyes all ablaze,
To find the best way
To get back at the pain
That was inflicted on them.
It seems that wasn't at all fair
That spite is needed
To hammer it home
That the fault was all theirs.
"Can't you see that?"
"I'm telling you so."
And retribution, funnily, agrees

That the situation requires
For all to see
That punishment is admired
When wrong-doing is done.
But what of the one
Who is spitting out spite,
Or the other who is banging their fist,
Oh, so loudly indeed,
That both spite and retribution
Suddenly turn to each other,
Quite startled, it seems,
As if woken from a stupor
With what they are doing,
They realise quite suddenly
Is hurting themselves
As much as the other.
For what are they gaining
By their fierce emotions
If all this vile energy
Is taken on board?
And it becomes startlingly clear
That their viscous expressions
Are showing very clearly
Their unhappiness is theirs
For not delving deeply,
No matter how ineptly,
And see the cavernous hole
That they have dug for themselves.
But pleases the ego so well!
For they couldn't see before
What can surely be seen now,
That their pain and retribution

Was what they thought correct,
When really it is guilt
That is blinding them so
For not being able
To view the complex arena
That they were a part of.
But it wasn't easy to see
In the maelstrom of life
That to do better
At the time
Was a futility for sure
Because it was beyond
Their comprehension.
To see it otherwise
But now very slowly
Both seem to agree
That spite and retribution
Will be of no help
When helping oneself
Discover their wounds
Will be a much better choice
Of energy expended.
So quietly they now reflect
That spite and retribution
Are not of immense value
When working to reveal
The wounds that are theirs.
To fondle and give care
To their wound fully explosed
Will serve them best now
To give them an insight
Of how sad the case was. 🥀

Homelessness

We are all homeless
At one time or another,
Even in our minds
If not in another.
But take a look closely
At the homeless we have,
Sitting on sidewalks,
And let's ask ourselves
Honestly,
Is that how it needs to be?
We have the money for fireworks
On New Year's Eve,
And everyone who is watching
Can admire the spectacle,
With the pretty flashing lights
That turn the night sky
Into a splatter of color,
While on the sidewalk nearby
Are homeless huddling
To keep out humanity
And wonder what all the fuss is about,
Because never have they
Experienced such gasps
From people walking past,
As they struggle to keep
Their few possessions intact.
What does it take
In our first world order

To see that it takes little
To house these sorry souls
That don't require much,
Nor are asking for much,
But do require shelter,
No matter how basic.
Surely a society such as ours
Needs to reflect rather deeply
To examine its conscience
And ask itself profoundly
That living on a street
Is not a real option
When most of us live
In our comfortable abodes.
Just as it takes a village
To raise a child,
Surely it must take a society
To support the destitute
And homeless.
For cannot we see
That the plight of the homeless
Is just a reflection
On the care in the community
Which seems rather deficient
In this world that has plenty
To spend on the excess
Of what we don't need.
But some may say rightly,
"I pay my taxes,
So I have done my bit,"
As if to say,
"I can wash my hands of that."

But it doesn't take much
To land on the street,
As many will attest.
But it doesn't really matter
If the homeless are few
Or embarrassingly too many,
The fact still remains
That addressed it is not,
And so we continue
Avoiding where at all possible
Eye contact with anyone
That appears homeless at all. ❧

Life is Magic

Life is magic,
Make the most of it.
Life is baffling,
Make the most of it.
Life is exhilarating,
Make the most of it.
Life is brutal,
Make the most of it.
Life is forgiving;
Learn to do the same.
Life is short;
Learn to ride with it.
Life is tedious;
Learn to embrace it.
Life is gracious;
Learn to be the same.
Life is memorable;
Learn to be memorable.
Life is funny;
Find the funny side.
Life is joy;
Where to find it?
Life is your guide;
Be guided.
And in the enormity of life,
Embrace it humbly,
And bow to its magnificence. ❧

Meditation

Meditation, you are so annoying,
That it is quite irritating,
As I wriggle and squirm
To sit and be quiet.
My mind is so racy;
It doesn't want to listen
To my admonitions
That it needs to adhere
To the silence
I'm trying to create within,
To give myself space
To align with stillness
And feel the uniqueness
That silence can bring.
I feel so agitated,
And frustration is mounting,
As this all seems so
Woo-woo and not entertaining.
I want to be free of this
Awful sensation,
Where my mind wants to wander
In directions so many.
They say persist
And It will happen,
That the quietness you are seeking
Will come about soon.
I want to complain about
My yesterday,
As it was not to my liking

And felt like striking
Someone not nice.
But as I contemplate
My dilemma indeed,
Suddenly out of nowhere
A peace seems to descend
Ever so quietly,
And maybe surreptitiously,
As my mind transcends
Suddenly through this chasm
Of silence remarkable,
And I feel a sensation
Like never before,
Where my mind, it appears, still,
And my body quieted now,
And it seems like a flower
Has bloomed deep inside of me.
Oh, how amazing is this
As I witness myself
Being able to submit
To this all-encompassing
Quietude
That fills me with awe
As never before.
And now I agree,
Persistence is a jewel
Which needs great acknowledgment
That meditation can achieve
The remarkable.
I agree
As I sit in deep reverence
In this beautiful silence. 🐾

Defenselessness

In my defenselessness,
My safety lies.
So states lesson 153
In my cherished book,
A Course in Miracles no less.
Oh, it is so good,
Profoundly inspiring.
We are led to believe
That defending ourselves
When we feel much threatened
And need to acknowledge
That we are not prepared
To move from our ground
Just creates anger
Multiplied.
For defending oneself
Will agitate the other
Who feels more than righteous
That they know the truth
Of what they are defending
So dreadfully vehemently.
But engaging in such
A useless discourse
With someone who has
Decided already
That they are absolutely right
And you have no chance
To have a voice here

It is best to step back
And observe most calmly
That nothing will come
Of this angry encounter
If you feel the necessity
To defend your opinion
Then ask yourself
Truthfully
What needs defending.
Because if we are comfortable
With our point of view
There is no need to defend
To start a useless row.
So walk away graciously
And let it be so
With honor intact
And heart wide open
To having averted
A situation dire
That had no possibility
To end with a smile. 🧩

Beauty

Beauty comes in a myriad of forms.
It is so overwhelming
Exhilarating and bedazzling
That in this world
Of so much excruciating pain
Where ugliness can abound
We have this magical contrast
That can mesmerise us so
With the beauty that flows
Out of so much in life.
From a voice that may
Express itself in such beautiful sound
That to hear it
Makes you pivot and listen.
Or music may transport you
To this, this out of body
Experience,
That feels so light
Light as floating on air.
It fills your body
With its vibrating melody,
That every cell in your body
Responds to the sound
And it feels ethereal
As you absorb this cadence
Of sound.
Just like in nature
Sound abounds

From the rustle of a leaf
To the crash of an ocean wave
Or the thunder that
Booms from the dark sky above.
There is beauty in all this
And if we stand so still
We can feel the pulsation
Of all this beauty around us
That penetrates like waves
Into the deepest corners
Of our beating heart,
As it takes on the wonder
That before it explodes
With the expression of a child
As it looks at you in wonderment
And adoration,
With such equanimity
Of love
That it becomes overwhelming
That a child's face can express
What adults may have forgotten.
That the beauty a face offers
Is straight from the soul
With such deep knowingness
It offers a plethora of wisdom
That beauty is in
Every eye and gesture.
Gather up this beauty
In all its forms
Breath it in deeply
And be transported away
To a place so delicate and light

That feeds the soul
And makes the heart whole.
And anchor this in
Your body so heavy
From the woes of the world
That it can give sustenance
And create quite a change
To a body that is weighed down
From this earth school of ours
That seems to give us
Little reprieve from its
Pounding refrains and strains
As it hobbles along
All battered and bruised.
So breath in deeply
Where beauty may be found
In the ladybird bug
That lands on you so,
Just to remind you
That you are beauty indeed
Personified 🧩

Accommodate

There goes a saying,
"Give me a child
To the age of seven,
Then I have them for life."
Job done,
Programs locked in
To be operated at will,
As the moment requires.
We know how to behave,
Just as manners hammered in well.
Our programs are set,
And we have accommodated
To the environment we live in.
It may be quite lovely
And seem rather nice,
But you make sure you please
To keep the peace,
Or you don't seem to be heard.
As the youngest of three,
So you make sure
You give everyone a laugh
So you are heard
As well as seen,
And that makes you feel
Significant indeed.
Or you may feel
From the verbal abuse
That you need to be perfect
To be acknowledged at all.

But strive as you might,
It never seems good enough,
And so one learns to
Accommodate so.
With the programs set for life,
Our path becomes rigid,
As we subconsciously
Live out our programs a-many.
And as adults, frustration builds
As we cannot extricate ourselves
From being the pleaser
Or accepting the abuse
That seems to follow us relentlessly
Wherever we go.
From the authoritarian boss
Who wants perfection no less,
Or the lover who expects
To be pleased all the way.
To realize we are running
A program at all
Takes some insight for sure,
With a fair few setbacks
As we start to contemplate
Or it's brought to our attention
That running these programs
Are not serving us well.
But to unpack these darn things
That have given us wrong comfort,
It becomes quite obvious
That the unpacking is
Laborious indeed,
Fraught with deep sorrow

That we have lived a life
As if like a robot,
But expecting life to turn out
As we had dreamed from the beginning.
To unpack these programs
Requires much digging
And delving in deep
And to give oneself freedom,
We must be courageous
And step out
Into territory less familiar
But very liberating
That we can discard being a pleaser
And abuse needs no longer
To be part of our life.
But then the unpacking seems endless indeed
As each new unpacking
Seems to reveal
That there is more to unpack with every viewing.
But please don't despair
As it's ever so rewarding
When we arrive at a place
That feels more at peace
And life is worth living
Without these rigid programs
So then the packing remaining
Just becomes part of growing
And learning to live well
In this world that throws curve balls a many.
But now we feel lighter
And wiser for certain
To handle this world with all its travails. 🧩

Flat line

Can you imagine
A flat line that goes on ad infinitum?
No ups or downs,
No ripples to this steady line
That some would have us call Life.
A flat line is safe;
There are no undulations,
No emotions out of place.
All neat and tidy,
No need to delve below the line
And find those elusive emotions
Locked away in a neat package
Without access or want
To see what could be in
That mysterious package
That seems rather heavy.
But don't be concerned
As it won't be opened
To peer inside,
As we can safely say
There is no need
As long as we travel along this
Flat line.
But what if the other
Would like to explore
What maybe is hidden inside
This package held tight?
Emotions need exploring

To see how to engage
Into the realms of one's life
So that we can live
More than a flat line.
But some would counter no doubt
A flat line is safe
And I want to keep it that way
For then I don't need to inquire
Which emotion fits with what occasion
As if an emotion needs pairing to an event
And not knowing how
This pairing would go
It's better by far
To go steady and safe
Along that flat line that is beautifully smooth.
Oh what a pity
One could say
When one wants a flat line
And the other wants to express
That causes a dilemma
With no easy solution
As both are at loggerheads
Demanding it their way.
There is no easy conclusion
In such an arena
Except allowing the one
Who wants to explore emotions
Grow their own wings
And fly to their freedom
Where restriction and confinement
Are no longer a part

Of their everyday life
And they can freely
Explore their emotions
With like-minded souls. 🧩

Probabilities and possibilities

Probability felt safe in its place in life
And had no intention
Of inquiring, what for?
Probability felt secure
That fate it was living
And clearly convinced
It was a good way to live.
For it took some of the angst out of
Ruminating over
That there could be
Possibilities around the next corner.
But fate seemed comforting
As then it could say,
"If things don't work out,
That it was set in my fate."
Fate can pull strongly
As it draws you in
To seal your life
In some mundane pattern.
And generations have lived by this mantra
That they like to convey
That the fate of this
Family has been set
Long ago.

But possibility shakes its head in amazement
And wonders why anyone
Would succumb
To their fate.
Better to do
A 90' turn
And go off the path
That fate thought it had sealed.
In this 90' turn
We can lose some of our baggage
And give us the chance
To explore exciting new horizons
That loom up to meet
Possibility's endeavor
To see how to live a life
Extraordinarily different
That the one fate may have chosen
For it to abide by.
Make a choice in life
To explore your possibilities
And leave behind probabilities
Together with fate.
Ah yes, there will be challenges
No doubt about that
On this road of possibilities
But then maybe just maybe
A new life will be had.

Silence

Ah silence my friend
What a beautiful interlude
You are to my heart
When nothing can be heard
But the beat of my heart.
You are so rich
With the potential
Of possibilities
When anything can emerge
From the bowels of silence.
It lingers in the air
With a profound emanation
Of peace and tranquility
As it holds me in deep Grace
And gives me the space
To ponder my life
In a humbling manner
For it asks nought of me
Nor expects a response
As I feel my way
Through this ever present
Beguiling refrain
From my friend deep silence
As it holds me gently
In its enrapt embrace
And I feel the magic
Of this silence so deep
That I dare not disturb it

For it feeds me so well
As it allows me to feel
Whatever I need
And that gives me
The time to gather my thoughts
And feel myself
Returning to whole
Once again
From the blaring menagerie
Of our bustling world
But silence is quite firm
That my time with it is precious
And makes sure
The banging and clattering
Of the world we all
Abide in
Is kept at a distance
As I enjoy my silence
To recharge my psyche
As tomorrow again
I will enter the fray
Of this relentless earth school
And will have to navigate
Another day out there
But while I can descend
Into my silence
Like into a calming hot bath
I will savour the enjoyment
Of being in silence
That is nourishing indeed 🧩

Rectification

As we travel our life
And get more entangled
In the obstacles that trip us so
With the twisted chaos
Within the heaviness of our heavy minds
And our bodies feel weary
Carrying this load
That ailments start to manifest
And our health can deteriorate
In untold ways.
For the tangled neurology
Gives signals galore
As life is not working out
In little ways and big
That we had hoped so sincerely.
And I know that there are many ways
To go and discover
What lies in our minds
Where things keep festering
And bubbling away
And creating quite the display
In a kaleidoscope of ways.
From symptoms of stomach aches
To mild depression
To explosive anger
To wanting to curl up in a ball
To relationship issues
To back aches as well

All of these and more
Hinder our life
In a myriad of ways.
And some of us go
On a long, long journey
To try and make sense
Of this mess we are in
And may find some satisfaction
From talking things through
And give us the relief
For at least understanding more
How we find ourselves
In such sticky waters
That make no sense at all.
But we still may be left
With running the same programs
As we tread the ground in frustration
For we haven't discovered the cause
Of these programs we run.
For try as we might
We find ourselves in
The same situations as before
Just with better understanding
How maybe to handle
What previously we had
No idea at all.
But being the practitioner that I am
And coming from the background
Where cause is the source
That must be found
It made so much sense
When NET was created

By a genius of a man.
And I could learn
How to get to the cause
Of anyone's pain
Be it in mind or in body
And alleviate it
With a simple procedure
Called NeuroEmotional Technique.
Now it isn't the panacea
And it's no miracle procedure
Although miracles abound
From this simple technique.
And people feel lighter
As if a load has been lifted
But more importantly still
It finds the root cause
Of so many dilemmas and traumas
That plague us so profoundly.
And we can step out of our programs
That have been running our lives
And leave behind the causes
That gave us no reprieve.
So thank you, Dr. Scott Walker
And Dr. Deb as well
For bringing to the world
Such a beautiful method
That has helped so many
To live better and more richly
For without this technique
We would be poorer by far
To understanding our mind
As we store in our body

Every experience we have had
From the time of conception
To our present time
Without exception
And not all our experiences
Serve us well
When we are trying to live our best life
Through our best selves.
But NET does help us discover
What lies underneath
And clear this brilliantly
So we truly can live
To our full potential
To be the miracle we are. 🧩

The road less traveled

Take the road less travelled
As Frost's poem begins
And Peck writes in his book.
For the fork in the road
Depicts an awareness indeed
That the road you choose
Is the rarer of the two
For it no longer is
Part of the beaten track
And must be forged
Alone with oneself.
And lonely it may be
At times that is certain
But eventually loneliness
Transmutes to a celebration
Of oneness with self
That is so liberating
On this journey as one.
For at times it is dark
On this track into oneself
That can become
Quite frightening.
For what will one find
And yes it may be ugly
That may be true
For some of those corners
Along this path dark
Are anything but pleasant

To face them and see
That we could have done better.
At times it is true
But we did do our best
At that time we can't deny
Because our wounds
Were a plenty
And they didn't have rein
With the rawness of the emotions
That flooded from them.
And that is why
As we travel
Along this road less travelled
It gives us the chance
To discover the cause
Of the wounds that ran deep
In days gone by.
And try as we might
Until we can evolve
There was no way we could resolve
These bleeding wounds of ours.
It's part of the journey
Of being so human
And being so flawed
That the only way forward
Is to find the Grace within
And have compassion
For the soul that you are.
That our ego elbows in
To cover the wound
That seems too painful
To examine and dissect

To clean it out well
And sew it up then.
To give us the chance
To resolve in ourselves
The trauma that plagued us
In years gone by.
To be able to emerge
From the darkened track
And discover a lightness of foot
That is altogether different
Than when we started
Many moons ago now.
And what a journey it's been
As we crawled at times
Through the mud that was so thick
That it took so much effort
To move slowly forward
With grit and determination
As we were not prepared to stay
In this dark of the road
That didn't seem friendly
As criticism blared
And our heart despaired
That our ego so strong
Was hard to let go.
But battle we did
As we moved quite slow
Along this road of ours
That was such a travail
Of wounds cleaned out
And ego discarded.

To step out into
The sunshine so bright,
To find that the journey
Along this road travelled
Was worthy indeed
Of our strident efforts.
And now we can feel
That we can go forth
With many more tools
To continue this journey
And feel better equipped
To handle the challenges
That this earth school of ours
Seems to offer us freely.
So go dear soul
And now embrace the road
As it comes up to meet you
As never before
Have you felt quite so ready
To embrace life itself
In its magical stream ✥

Lessons

Lessons are a plenty
As we travel along
This road called Life.
At times it seems
Rather nice
As we seem to be going along quite well,
Or so it seems
Along this winding track.
That we seem to navigate well
When all of a sudden
We are caught unawares
As we erupt into an altercation
From we know not where,
With someone dear to us.
It wasn't planned;
We are emphatic about that!
But a trigger it seems
Was detonated reflexly
And there is no way emphatically
That we are going to let this
Situation pass
Without our say.
We fire away as the other does as well,
Only to be left
Feeling empty inside
Because what did we achieve
In going hell for leather
To stand our ground?

But determined we were
To make it known
That our point of view
Is significant indeed
Which it might well be.
But standing our ground
And making sure we are heard
Achieves nothing for us,
Them, or the future.
For any trigger which is ours
Needs to be owned
As ours indeed,
As something in us
Is the source of this woe
That we need to own
And find its true cause.

But they 'made' me mad
Oh, how frustrating are they,
And all one wants to do
Is make them see that.
But it still doesn't resolve
That we were triggered so,
And need to delve into us
To understand this.
At times it may feel
Quite futile and upsetting,
As we dig and still don't find
The source of our trigger.
But at other times,
As we peer into this deep crevice
Of ours, we call past

We may eventually see
The connection with past and present.
If that is the case,
We can learn to heal
This past wound of ours
That led us to be triggered
In our present altercation.
For when we heal this wound
Of the past,
We are no longer triggered
By a present situation,
And can magnanimously
Allow it to be.
For nothing is ever solved
Coming from our triggers,
But much is gained
If we can hold our own
And also compassion for the other,
To either walk away without a qualm,
Or find how in unison
You can both
Embrace the dilemma
And resolve it from a higher perspective

Sorry

Sorry seems to be
The hardest word to say,
As Elton John sings
In his melancholy song.
We may find it so hard to
Admit we are wrong,
Because our ego
Is jumping up and down.
"Don't lower yourself so"
It says, and "say you are sorry
When the other should
Be saying the sorry".
But then again,
We may be quick to blurt out
At any small thing
That we seem to think
Has impacted the other.
For we cannot see,
Due to our own set of fears,
That sorry can be
Such a sad word indeed,
When it is ourselves
We need to be forgiving.
For we see ourselves in such a poor light
That surely an apology
Will set it all right.
What can I say
But neither is right,

When if it comes from a place
Where fear is might.
Let us first get to know
Why we either bow
Immediately so,
Or stand quite rigid
To defend our stand so.
We usually come from a place of deep pleasing
Or defiant rebellion,
Due to our wounds from the past
Where we did our best
To find a way through
Those childhood travails
That left us in dismay
Of how best to protect
Our inept selves.
For in childhood, we choose
A method that seems
To work for the arena
We find ourselves in.
But until we address
Where this mind accommodation began,
We will be none the wiser
For what to do now.
So reflect on your past deeply
And follow the dots back
To the place where it all started
To realise its worth
In the environment we were in.
It then becomes a liberation indeed
To discover we can become
More discerning - oh wow,

And learn to say sorry
In a meaningful way
That carries the weight
That is so deserves.
For now we know how
To apologise wisely
And feel a freedom in this,
That is so enlightening 🧩

Control and manage

Control is acted out
In a plethora of ways,
And so we may perceive
Our way of being
In this world we call home
Is not being in control
By our standards at all.
But we do like things to be
Nice and tidy, no doubt,
Everything having its place,
Perfect and well set out,
Which is reassuring
And feels so efficient,
Without a doubt.
But to what extent are we needing
To have everything so,
And are we prepared
For it to be
Not quite so?
We may have a messy home,
Office, or room,
But our mind needs all the schedules
To be just so,
And to know it is all correct
And operating according to plan.
For without a plan and schedule,
We feel quite unstable.
But no one has informed us

Or we haven't been taught
That within or without,
Fear
Is lurking in these minds of ours,
That whether our external space
Or our world in our head,
Things need to be
Without any doubt,
Well thought out
And confirmed and controlled.
But what of the flip side
If we become aware
That controlling anything
Becomes very fatiguing?
And if we learn to
Let go of this fear
As we learn to understand
Why we need such control,
We begin to realize
That there is freedom in letting go,
And concede that learning
To manage
Is not nearly as taxing.
But we first need to view
And let go of our fear
That whether in or without,
That fear needs to be understood.
And then when this process
Has cleared our fear,
We can learn that managing
Is so liberating.
For then there is flexibility

In how we approach
All aspects of our life,
And feel more in charge
Than ever before.
And now understand clearly
That fear was the driving force
Behind our control. 🧩

Love

What an exhilarating feeling of being in love.
It can fill us with awe
And such great expectations
It can make the world look
Like a sparkling panorama
That has no end on the vistas of horizons
That keep flooding our being
With infinite wonderment.
When love emanates from our heart
And courses every fiber of our being,
And we feel so alive,
We can conquer anything
And be everyone's friend.
For the feeling takes our breath away
And gives us a smile
That radiates wonderment
Towards our lover or child.
And all seems well with the world.
But what of the person
Who has never experienced
Such a deep, deep feeling
Or it has been ripped away
As life can do
Or fades surreptitiously
With the march of time?
And we are left bewildered
So sad and bereft
That suddenly or slowly or never it seems

Have we felt so destitute
And so very alone
When love no longer
Courses our veins
And bursts from our heart.
We put such emphasis on external love
That when it is no longer there
To lift us up high,
We flounder and sink into a deep state of agony
Of where to find that next fix of love
To feel alive again and have meaning in life.
But friend, we need to turn around
And look at the one - who we are
And ask ourselves honestly,
Have we loved ourselves at all
Or sought satisfaction from our external world?
For first we must learn to love ourselves so
That we are blinded by the being we are
And find within that uniqueness of self
That fills us with awe
At how beautiful we are
In the essence of us.
So find that deep place within
So that the smile that emanates
Is truly from one who has found true love
In the magnificence of you 🧩

Listening

When one asks another
What they have been doing
Or what their thoughts may be
On one thing or another,
Listening becomes the paramount action
That we need be acting out.
For in listening with laser ears,
We give the other the honor of ourselves
To every nuance of inflection
That the other is expressing.
With such listening,
We will no doubt discover
Not only what they have been doing
But also how they are feeling
As they are relating
A part of their life
That is important to them.
And remember you did ask.
To respect another such
Gives us the opportunity to see
How much we respect ourselves
And how well we are able
To listen to who we are
When we are conversing
With none other than oneself.
For in listening to another
Without preparing a response in our heads
Before the other has completed

What seemed to be asked in earnest,
Gives us such depth of knowledge
To really experience
The fullness of the other.
It takes deep reflection within ourselves
To be able to be present
In such a manner.
For as we get to know who we are
And understand somewhat
What we are in essence,
Only then are we able to give the same to the other.
And the art of listening well
Becomes quite revelatory.
For now our heart can beat in that instant
To the rhythm of the other

www.ingramcontent.com/pod-product-compliance
Lightning Source LLC
Chambersburg PA
CBHW051038050426
42335CB00049B/419